DRAWING UNEXPLAINED- MYSTERY MONSTERS

ILLUSTRATED BY JANOS JANTNER

PowerKiDS press.

New York

Published in 2013 by The Rosen Publishing Group, Inc.
29 East 21st Street, New York, NY 10010

First Edition

Produced for Rosen by Calcium Creative Ltd
Editors: Sarah Eason and Rosie Hankin
Editor for Rosen: Sara Antill
Book Design: Paul Myerscough

Illustrations by Janos Jantner

Library of Congress Cataloging-in-Publication Data

Jantner, Janos.
 Drawing unexplained-mystery monsters / by Janos Jantner. — 1st ed.
     p. cm. — (How to draw monsters)
 Includes index.
  ISBN 978-1-4777-0312-0 (library binding) —
  ISBN 978-1-4777-0346-5 (pbk.) — ISBN 978-1-4777-0347-2 (6-pack)
 1. Monsters in art—Juvenile literature. 2. Animals, Mythical, in art—Juvenile
literature. 3. Drawing—Technique—Juvenile literature. I. Title.
 NC825.M6J363 2013
 743'.87—dc23
                                              2012026380

Manufactured in the United States of America

CPSIA Compliance Information: Batch #W13PK7: For Further Information contact Rosen Publishing, New York, New York at 1-800-237-9932

CONTENTS

UNEXPLAINED MONSTERS

From giant apes and underwater serpents, to deadly worms and bloodsucking beasts, people love to be scared by tales of mysterious monsters! Now you can bring your very own terrifying monsters to life through art!

YOU WILL NEED

Just a few simple pieces of equipment are needed to create awesome monster drawings:

Sketchpad or paper
Visit an art store to buy good quality paper.

Pencils
A range of drawing pencils are essential. You will need both fine-tipped and thick-tipped pencils.

Eraser
You can remove any unwanted lines with an eraser, and you can even use it to add highlights.

Paintbrush, paints, and pens
Buy a set of quality paints, brushes, and coloring pens to add color to your monster drawings.

MONSTER FACTS

Once you've created your amazing mystery monsters, find out more about the terrifying beasts by checking out great monster facts!

BIGFOOT

This fearsome monster looks like a giant ape and is said to have been seen in the wilderness of North America, Asia, and Australia. The beast is named for the huge footprints it leaves behind. In a newspaper report written in 1851, two hunters described the beast threatening a flock of sheep. Over the years, other terrifying tales have been told.

STEP 1

Use rectangles and ovals to roughly draw your creature's trunk, head, arms, legs, hands, and feet.

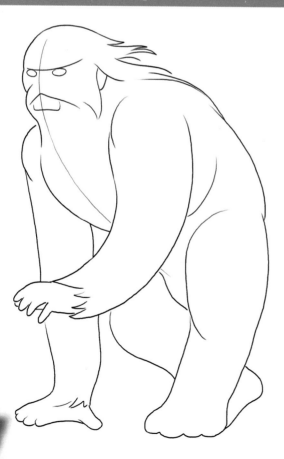

STEP 2

Draw over your shapes to create the beast's outline. Erase the shapes you drew in step 1. Then begin to draw parts of the face, fingers, and fur.

STEP 3

Now you can begin to add more detail. Pencil lines for the fur on the monster's face, head, neck, shoulders, chest, back, arms, and legs. Add fingernails to the hands and sharp claws to the feet. Focus on the face, too. Add a snarling mouth and a small nose. Draw the shape of the eyes. Then add some muscle lines to the beast's chest.

STEP 4

Use a fine-tipped pencil to add even more lines of fur. Draw the creature's hairy body, from its head to its toes. Then add detail to the eyes and the knuckles of the hands. Don't forget to add some terrifying teeth!

STEP 5

Now add some shading to the face, neck, arms, waist, and legs. By shading your picture you will help to show how big and bulky your scary monster is!

STEP 6

Begin to color your creature. Use a palette of dark brown for the fur, and light brown for the skin. Add some pink lips and piercing light blue eyes. Use ivory for the teeth and monster's nails.

STEP 7

Now add white highlights to the beast's skin and fur to give it more depth. Use fine strokes to color the shaggy coat. Light tints will also help show the big muscles of the chest, the pointed edges of the teeth, and the razor-sharp claws.

MONSTER FACT!

Many people think that Bigfoot is a myth. But some scientists believe this creature could be a relative of an ancient giant ape that lived over a million years ago. This beast, named *Gigantopithecus*, was 10 feet (3 m) tall!

9

SCARY GHOST

For thousands of years, many people have believed in ghosts. They claim to have seen the spirit of a dead person or animal. Ghosts are said to haunt places or people they knew in life.

STEP 1

To create your ghost, draw ovals for the head, arms, and lower body. Use rectangles for the neck, trunk, and hands.

STEP 2

Draw a fine line over the outline and erase your rough shapes from step 1. Add hair, fingers, and parts of the face.

STEP 3

Now focus on the ghost's dress. Pencil the top section so it sits on either side of the collarbone. Then add loose, flowing sleeves fastened with a button. Keep the skirt fabric long and wispy. Draw the ghost's fingers. Add more strands of hair. Then introduce a few more lines to the face.

STEP 4

Use a fine-tipped pencil to add even more strands of hair. Put some creases in the flowing fabric. Add some detail to the eyes and draw the neck. Fill the mouth with teeth.

STEP 5

Now add shading to the hair, face, neck, and underside of the sleeves. Shade the inner sleeves and the folds of the dress. Keep the bottom of the dress light and wispy.

STEP 6

Use a palette of pink and brown for the skin and hair. Then put a wash of purple over the dress. Use dark tints for the dress top and sleeves, then very light tints for the lower dress.

STEP 7

Now add some white highlights to bring your ghost to life! Light tints on the skin will add more depth. Highlights on the dress will show how delicate the folds are. Keep the bottom of the dress very light and pale, as if it is about to disappear!

MONSTER FACT!

Ghosts are often described as misty. This belief may come from ancient times when a person's spirit was linked to their breath. When you breathe out on a cold day, your breath can be seen as a white mist. People once believed this was a person's spirit.

LOCH NESS MONSTER

This enormous creature is said to live in Loch Ness. This is a large lake in the Scottish Highlands, in the UK. In 1933, newspaper reports told of a giant fish or sea serpent living in the depths of the loch. Many people traveled to Scotland to look for the beast, now nicknamed "Nessie."

STEP 1

Draw ovals to create Nessie's head and body. Then use triangles for the fins and long, sweeping curved lines for the neck and tail.

STEP 2

Pencil the monster's outline, then erase the shape lines from step 1. Begin to draw the features of the face.

STEP 3

Now add pencil lines to show Nessie's ribs, and draw the curves of the neck, tail, and four fins. Add more detail to the gaping mouth, eyes, and brow. Notice how long the neck and tail are compared to the rest of the body. Notice, too, how the serpent's jaws are wide open!

STEP 4

It's time to add some razor-sharp teeth to Nessie's jaws. This is a monster you don't want to meet in the water! Add detail to the tongue and snout. Then draw more creases on the skin of the neck, chest, and tail.

STEP 5

Now add some shading for a 3D effect. Shade the inside of the gaping mouth, the underside of the neck, and beneath the fins. Shading will give the belly and tail more depth, too.

STEP 6

Use a palette of light blue, gray, and white for Nessie's skin. Add shades of red for the tongue and open jaws. Nessie's colors help it to stay camouflaged in the water.

STEP 7

Complete your image by adding cream highlights to your creature. Light tints on the snout will emphasize the bumpy skin. Highlights on the head, neck, belly, back, tail, and fins will add more depth. Don't forget to highlight the sharp points of those terrible, daggerlike teeth!

MONSTER FACT!

Descriptions of the Loch Ness Monster paint a picture of a creature much like ancient reptiles named plesiosaurs. These creatures lived at the same time as the dinosaurs. They had small heads and long, slim necks. However, scientists think it is unlikely a plesiosaur could survive in Loch Ness.

MONGOLIAN DEATH WORM

Found in the Gobi Desert in Asia, this monster has been described as a bright red worm with a body up to 60 inches (150 cm) long. It is known as a terrible killer that sprays a deadly poison and gives off a sharp electric shock. The beast hibernates underground for most of the year. It is said to then come to the surface in June and July, when the ground is wet after rainfall.

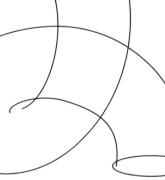

STEP 1

Use circles and tubes to roughly draw your Death Worm's body. Draw a long tube shape for the body and two circles for the head. Draw a large circle, then a smaller one within it.

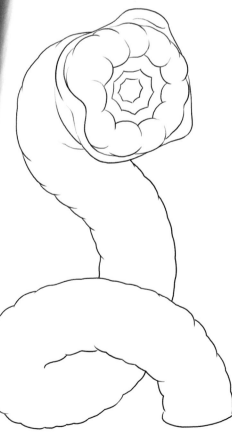

STEP 2

Draw a finer pencil outline, then erase the lines made in step 1. Begin to add detail to the creature's strange snout.

STEP 3

Now use a fine-tipped pencil to add more detail to your beast. Draw four tentacles reaching out from the sides of the head. Draw the ridges of the squirming body. Then add some detail to the strange, sucker-like mouth crammed full of super-sharp teeth.

STEP 4

Add some detail to the sand surrounding your Death Worm. Imagine it burrowing out of the ground in search of victims! Add some more fine lines to the neck and wriggling body.

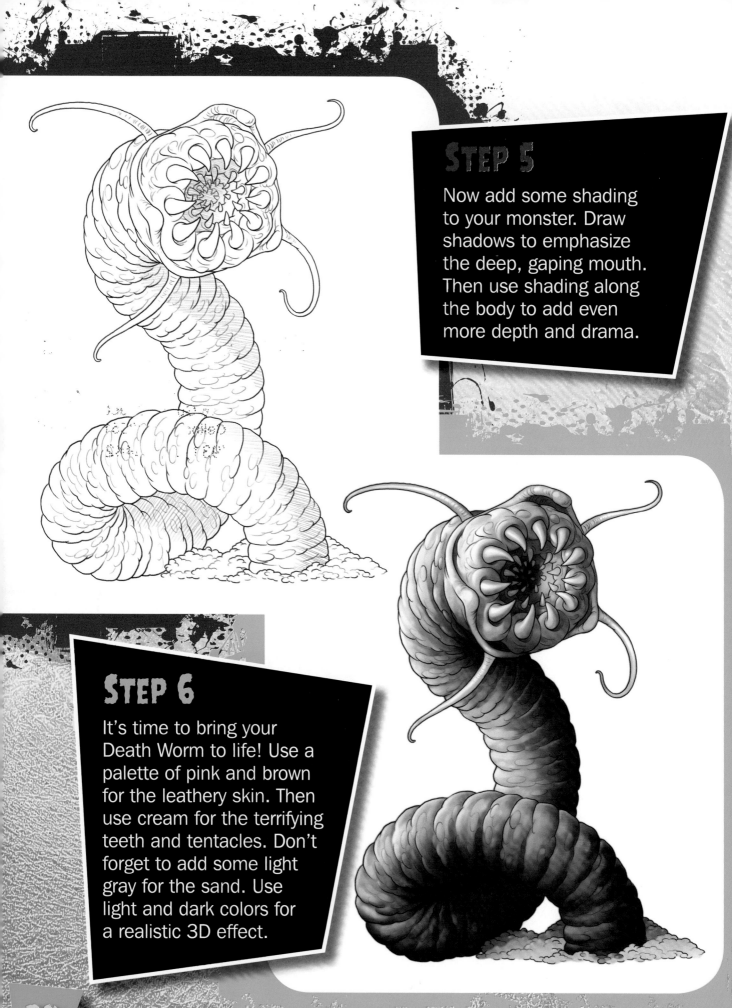

STEP 5

Now add some shading to your monster. Draw shadows to emphasize the deep, gaping mouth. Then use shading along the body to add even more depth and drama.

STEP 6

It's time to bring your Death Worm to life! Use a palette of pink and brown for the leathery skin. Then use cream for the terrifying teeth and tentacles. Don't forget to add some light gray for the sand. Use light and dark colors for a realistic 3D effect.

STEP 7

Now for some finishing touches. Add highlights to your creature's tentacles. Then focus on the curves of the sucker-like mouth. Light tints on the neck and body will add more depth. Don't forget to highlight the teeth, and the lumps and bumps of the body.

MONSTER FACT!

In 1926, American scientist Professor Roy Chapman Andrews heard tales of the fearsome Death Worm. He then described the giant creature in his book *On the Trail of Ancient Man*.

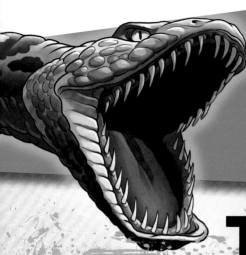

GIANT ANACONDA

The anaconda is one of the world's largest and deadliest snakes. It is said that giant anacondas swim in the rivers of South America. When Europeans began to explore the South American jungles, they told tales of a serpent that measured up to 148 feet (45 m) in length.

STEP 1

Draw rough curved lines to show the outline of your deadly snake's body. Then use a triangle and two rectangular shapes for the head and huge, gaping mouth.

STEP 2

Pencil the monster's outline, then erase the lines from step 1. Draw the coiled body and add some features to the face, too.

STEP 3

Draw some pencil lines to emphasize the curves of the long neck. Now begin to add more detail to the face, too. Include an eye and the edges of the mouth.

STEP 4

Add some more fearsome features! Fill the mouth with backward-facing teeth. Add detail to the evil eye. Then use a fine-tipped pencil to draw the ridges of the neck and belly.

23

STEP 5

Add a camouflage pattern to your snake's skin. Then shade the roof of the mouth, and the lumps and bumps of the head. Use shading to emphasize the curves of the slippery body.

STEP 6

Use a palette of green, blue, brown, and gray for your snake's camouflage. This cunning creature will catch you unawares! Use a lighter shade for the underside of the neck and belly. Don't forget a dark red for the menacing mouth.

STEP 7

Finally, add some white highlights to your monster's head, neck, and body to create even more depth. Give the shimmering, slippery body a smooth sheen. Then emphasize the lumpy head, and pointed teeth. Add a glint to the anaconda's evil eye. Your monster snake is complete!

MONSTER FACT!

Today, anacondas usually grow up to 33 feet (10 m) long. They are not poisonous creatures, but they are certainly deadly! Anacondas are a type of constrictor. This is a snake that coils its body around its victim, then squeezes it to death.

CHUPACABRA

Known as "goat-suckers," these creatures are said to live in the lands of North, South, and Central America. They are the size of a small bear and have leathery skin. Spines run along the Chupacabra's back, from its neck to the tail. Chupacabras were first reported in 1995 in Puerto Rico, after a flock of sheep had been attacked. The sheep had deep wounds to their chests and had been drained of all their blood.

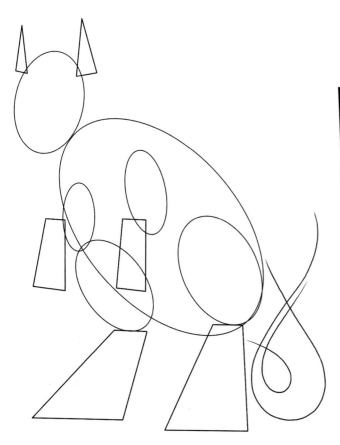

STEP 1

Draw ovals and rectangles for the creature's head, body, arms, and legs. Use triangles for the ears, and add the curves of the tail.

STEP 2

Pencil the monster's outline, then erase the shape lines from step 1. Begin to add detail to the face, paws, feet, and claws.

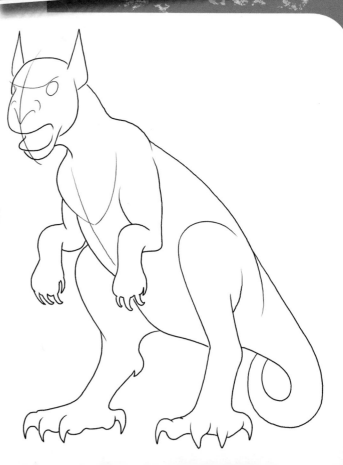

STEP 3

Now add spiky spines to your beast's back, head, and tail. Add more detail to the face. Include a snarling mouth, a heavy brow, and a wide-set jaw. Add some fur to the neck. Then draw the daggerlike claws.

STEP 4

Use a fine-tipped pencil to add more detail to your monster. Draw webs of skin between the spines. Then add wrinkles to the tail. Fill the mouth with razor-sharp teeth, and give the fur a soft, shaggy feel. Draw the nose. Then add pupils to the scary eyes.

STEP 5

By shading parts of the body, you will start to give your creature a 3D effect. Shade the ears, brow, neck, and belly. Then focus on the feet, legs, arms, and tail. This will add more depth.

STEP 6

Use a palette of brown, gray, and cream for your beast. Use dark shades for the leathery back, and lighter shades for the belly. Don't forget the pink lips, yellow eyes, and grizzly gray teeth. Then add some hairs to the muzzle.

STEP 7

Now add some light tints of color. Use white highlights on the face, neck, arms, legs, and belly. Light tints will also help to define the pointed ears, spiky spines, sharp teeth, and deadly claws. Add a glint to the evil eyes and a sheen to the swishing, swiping tail.

MONSTER FACT!

In 2010, American scientist Barry O'Connor suggested that Chupacabra attacks could have been the work of hungry coyotes infected by parasites. These sick dogs would have had little fur and thickened skin and might have looked like the descriptions of the Chupacabra.

GLOSSARY

ancient (AYN-shent) Very old, from a long time ago.

ape (AYP) A type of monkey.

brow (BROW) A ridge over the eyes.

burrowing (BUR-oh-ing) Digging or tunneling underground.

camouflaged (KA-muh-flahjd) Disguised, usually with color.

coiled (KOYLD) Wound around something in rings or circles.

coyotes (ky-OH-teez) Wolflike dogs that live in packs.

detail (dih-TAYL) The fine pencil markings on a drawing.

drama (DRAH-muh) Excitement and exciting events.

electric shock (ih-LEK-trik SHOK) An electric current passed through the body.

fins (FIHNZ) Parts of an animal's body used for swimming.

flock (FLOK) A group of animals, such as sheep or birds.

haunt (HAWNT) When a ghost visits a place regularly.

hibernates (HY-bur-naytz) Rests for a number of months.

highlights (HY-lytz) Light parts.

muzzle (MUH-zel) The nose and mouth area of an animal's face.

myth (MITH) A very famous, ancient story.

palette (PA-lit) A range of colors.

parasites (PER-uh-syts) Organisms that live in or on other organisms.

poison (POY-zun) A deadly substance.

puncture wounds (PUNGK-cher WOONDZ) When the skin is pierced by a sharp object.

relative (REH-luh-tiv) A person or creature from the same family.

reptiles (REP-tylz) Scaly skinned and cold-blooded creatures.

Scottish Highlands (SKAH-tish HY-lindz) An area in Scotland.

serpent (SUR-pent) A large snake.

shading (SHAYD-ing) Pencil lines that add depth to a picture.

snout (SNOWT) An animal's nose.

spirit (SPIR-ut) A person's "soul."

tentacles (TEN-tih-kulz) Parts of an animal's body used for grasping, moving, or feeling.

victims (VIK-timz) People who are killed or harmed in some way.

FURTHER READING

Pipe, Jim. *Ghosts*. The Twilight Realm. New York: Gareth Stevens, 2013.

Roberts, Steven. *Bigfoot!*. Jr. Graphic Monster Stories. New York: PowerKids Press, 2013.

Schach, David. *The Loch Ness Monster*. The Unexplained. Minneapolis, MN: Bellwether Media, 2011.

WEBSITES

Due to the changing nature of Internet links, PowerKids Press has developed an online list of websites related to the subject of this book. This site is updated regularly. Please use this link to access the list: www.powerkidslinks.com/htdm/myste/

INDEX